Freedom

From the Bondage of Brokenness

Andrée M. Harris.

Andree Harris Productions, LLC.

Parish Turn Ct

Virginia Beach, VA 22664

(202) 630-7323

www.andreeharrisproductions.com

Ordering Information: Quantity sales- Special discounts are available on quantity purchases by corporations, associations, and other entities. For details, contact the publisher.
For orders by U.S. trade bookstores and wholesalers, contact publisher.

Printed in the United States of America

Library of Congress Catalog in Publications Number:

2021942103

ISBN-13: 978-1-7350129-0-2 This book was printed in the
United States. All Scripture quotes are taken from the Holy
Bible, King James Version, Cambridge, 1769

To book Andrée M. Harris to speak at your event, please
contact info@andreemharris.com.

Table of Contents

Introduction 6

Chapter 1:Forgiveness 9

Chapter 2:Finding Your Way To Self-Love 15

Chapter 3:Accepting Yourself Just As You Are 20

Chapter 4:Trust The Transition During Times Of Change 26

Chapter 5:Find A Peaceful Place 33

Chapter 6:Overcome Fear And Improve Confidence 39

Chapter 7:Triumphing Over Tough Times 43

Chapter 8:Press Under Pressure 47

Chapter 9:Lonely But Not Alone 49

Chapter 10:Pursue Your Purpose In Life 55

Chapter 11:Overcoming Distractions 60

Chapter 12:When It Seems Like Its Over 64

Chapter 13:Stopping The Blame Game 70

Chapter 14:Dare To Dream 77

Chapter 15:The Power Of Prayer 80

Conclusion 85

About The Author 90

Dedication

I dedicate this book to people who remained in bondage and believed that absolute freedom would come one day.

Introduction

This book is a spin-off of my book titled Being Made Whole.

Free: Not under control or in the power of another and no longer confined or imprisoned, not restrained.

Brokenness: Having been fractured or damaged andno longer in one piece or working order.

Broken—that was the exact place where I was. Everything around me seemed to break apart—the church, marriage, health, home, finances, and relationships. I mean and everything! I could not seem to pull it together. I was among people and still felt lonely. I was in my 15th year of preaching when it hit me! I kept hearing, "you are a prisoner." It played over and over in my head. I thought about many things, but being in bondage and broken was not one of them. I had to get out of this place. I was suffocating, unbeknownst to many. I hosted workshops, empowerment calls, and revivals on breaking the chains, but chains and handcuffs were all over me.

Broken—yet, I still could encourage others. My saying used to be, "it's not about me." Let me take care of God's work, and God will surely take care of me. The thoughts in my mind did not line up with what I knew. For a moment, I walked away from it all. I was like a kid who had been kept in the house under a watchful eye for years. I developed hidden resentments against the church and several people who betrayed my trust, and my get back was to get into anything and everything. I had destructive behaviors with justifications that only sounded good to me.

I soon discovered that the picture-perfect life of fun that I thought I was having was quite the opposite.

The cocky behavior did not last long. My conscience was kicking in, and I began to feel uneasy. It was time for me to face the harsh reality. I was spiritually and emotionally broken, bitter, and bankrupt. I was in bondage, even though I thought I was free. I questioned God because it seemed like the closer I was to God, the worse things started happening around me. I began to live in regret, anger, and resentment. No matter what methods I tried to get relief from those feelings, they remained with me.

I did not see my life going in another direction until I learned how to sit still with myself (that is not always comfortable, believe me). I had to sit still long enough to allow my heart, mind, and eyes to become open to the possibility of change. As a result of my hurt, brokenness, and bitterness, I could not wrap my mind around anything positive. After an emotional breakdown, my spiritual dad felt that the time had come to share some transparency of his own life. He shared with me the highs, lows, and mistakes. I was in awe! I supposed it was because I rarely met anyone transparent enough to share what I had gone through. Not only that, he began to remind me of who I was. It had nothing to do with religious views. He encouraged me to get back to that place where I knew I could be. He told me that if I were to let go of the past and treat the present with hope for the future, I would surely win.

You can be free from the bondage of brokenness too. Allow yourself time to heal and deal. We are not perfect. We are just perfectly here for a purpose. My goal is to continue to live a life free of regrets. We cannot change the past, but we can play an essential role in our future if we only accept ourselves. We are a work in progress, and there is nothing too hard for God. This book provides positive steps to become free from bondage. Thank you for allowing me to share this journey with you. Together, we can be free.

CHAPTER 1

FORGIVENESS

Forgiveness of others and forgiveness of self is absolutely essential if you are to progress spiritually and reunite with your True Self. Unforgiveness binds you energetically to the other person and your lower self/ego.

Along life's path, we all encounter situations that hurt and causes us pain. It can be difficult or seemingly impossible to forgive the ones who have caused us such pain or committed heinous acts against us. Many of these situations strongly engage our emotions and energies, which in turn creates an energy matrix (pattern). Although unseen, these matrixes are every bit as real as any physical object on earth. They will stay intact until the situation is resolved or the energies are transmmited. This locks some of your energy in the past, many times to your own detriment. Although, the past is dead and gone, you kept it "alive" by non-resolution of the matter. At best, it sits there and festers. If you continued to bring up these situations and keep going over them in your mind, you feed the energy matrix and cause it to grow stronger. When my husband made a decision to walk away from our marriage,

I wanted him to feel the pain that I felt. Every time I thought about the situation, I would get angry.

By the Universal Law of Attraction this in turn attracts like energy to you in turn based on what you are outputting emotionally concerning to the incident. If you are angry, anger returns to you, multiplying and fueling the original energy output. This energy can affect you on physical, emotional and mental levels. The non-resolution of the issue continues to link you to many other situations. It will karmically bind you to any others involved until the situation is resolved.

Key-point: Until you truly forgive someone or something, you are bound to that situation or person.

Forgiveness of self may be the most difficult of all.

The other aspect of forgiveness - the forgiveness of oneself - can prove to be the most difficult of all. We can be our own worst enemies because we keep going over the all the misdeeds and wrongs we have committed. Many times as a result of the unforgiveness of self we subconsciously end up sabotaging things in our life as punishment. It is essential that we include forgiveness of self along with forgiving of others.

Forgive and Forget

Sometimes we are told that we must "forgive and forget." In truly forgiving someone or something, you do not need to forget the incident. However, you do *Let It Go* and realize that you don't have to forget it. You can still acknowledge that you or someone else did something 'wrong,' while at the same time forgiving.

Many times, the ego wants the other person to be punished or see justice prevail before truly forgiving and letting go. Knowing and understanding the Law of Karma (also known as the Law of Cause and Effect) is very helpful in letting go. It states that for every action there will be an equal and opposite reaction; which means that if you give happiness, you will received happiness in return. If you give sorrow, you will received sorrow in return. In other words, "as you sow, so shall you reap." The Law of Karma is indisputable and unerring. Thus you may know that Divine Justice will prevail.

Keys to Forgiving and Letting Go

How do you go through this process of forgiveness and letting go? This can be particularly hard if you have been involved in a traumatic situation. Understand that sometimes there is a part of the self that is responsible for these types of acts. It is known as the "Enemy Within." It has been called many names throughout the centuries such as the "Dweller on the Threshold" (Dweller), "the Anti-Self," and much more. Have you ever wondered why sometimes you do things that you know are wrong? Do you wonder why in the world you would ever do anything like that? Well that is due to the enemy! Everything that conflicts with good is an operation of the enemy. It prevent you from taking actions which would be better ones.

Understanding that there is this enemy within us was a major key for me personally, in finally being able to forgive and release things. It allowed me to see that there is a part of me that can be judged, condemned and not forgiven. Many on a spiritual path understand the need for forgiveness, but fall short of being able to do so. It is because they have the false concept that by forgiving they are excusing the offender for his/her behavior. They do not understand that forgiveness is necessary for spiritual growth. They tend to be forgiving on one hand, but lawful judgmental and prejudice on the other. So if you find it hard to forgive others for wrongs committed against you, then you should understand that forgiveness is truly for your peace but not for the offenders.

Set the "Forgiveness Blueprint"

Some of your issues of unforgiveness may involve incidents that happened years ago. The matrix that was established by going over and over these situations in your mind can be very powerful. At times, you can even become addicted to the pain and suffering that you feel when you relieve these events. That is why it is necessary to set a new matrix. Set a "Forgiveness

Blueprint" by having a clear intention and commitment to resolve the situation by forgiveness. This commitment must come from the core of your being - from your heart. Once you commit from your heart and state your clear intention to forgive, the power of that energy will begin to undo and shatter the old matrix. At the same time, it will establish a new blueprint for forgiving.

How Do You Know, You Have Forgiven?

When you meet the situation or person in your mind and the sting is no longer there, you know that you have successfully forgiven. One analogy would be having a painful abcess a year ago; the memory is still there, but the pain has been forgotten. You may know then that you have released the person or situation and are no longer bound. You are free from the entrapment of unforgiveness.

Practical Steps of Forgiveness:

1. List those situations in your life where you have not fully forgiven yourself or others. Examine each situation and ask yourself why you have not been able to forgive the persons involved in the situations. Try to see where your own hardness of heart, resentment or pride could be contributing to your unforgiveness of others.

2. Establish a new "Forgiveness Blueprint" for each situation of unforgiveness.

3. Pray and ask for help to establish a merciful heart for the complete forgiveness of self and others.

4. Apply the above process in "Key to forgiving and letting go" to every unresolved situation in your life.

CHAPTER 2

FINDING YOUR WAY TO SELF-LOVE

It's the puzzle we all face as we go about healing and restoring a wounded self-esteem. We want to value and love ourselves more completely. We certainly know the anguish when those old feelings of worthlessness creep in. We even know the areas where we are most "sensitive" and "self-critical."

But how on earth do we get from these wincing, self-negating feelings to feelings of self-love? How do we love ourselves when in many ways we so painfully do not?

If you are experiencing this frustration, do not be discouraged. In finding your way to self-love, it will often seem like "you just can't get there from here." This apparent impasse is absolutely to be expected.

Here's why. To feel love and to feel that healthy sense of self, we must first feel full and nourished. The problem, of course, is that self-negating feelings prevent us from being properly fed and filled. This is particularly true when these wounded feelings run deeply to our sense of self, our self-image and our very identity. Because we primarily "see" ourselves through this wounding as not enough (not "perfect" enough, not "thin" enough, not "accomplished" enough, not "together" enough, etc.). We deprive ourselves of that fundamental ongoing nourishment we need to experience that sense of being enough.

Here comes our double mind. We cannot see our worthiness to be filled and we cannot fill ourselves to see our worthiness. How do we get there from here?

The Bridge to Self-Love

Fortunately, there is an intermediate step, a "position" that bridges the divide between that deficit state of self-rejection and your natural full sense of self and self-love. It's a position that helps us begin to be nourished, despite the self-negating feelings, so we are able to revive and reawaken that innate sense of being okay and being enough.

The intermediate position is self-acceptance and self-compassion. Unlike that mysterious, far away land of self-love, this intermediate position is surprisingly easy to find and powerful.

Self-acceptance and compassion is not about trying to convince yourself that you are beautiful or successful (or whatever), when your wounded feelings are currently telling you that you're not. It's certainly not about exhausting yourself trying to fix what's "wrong" with you so that you satisfy that harsh and perfectionistic view. Neither of these responses do much to nourish you.

Moving into this intermediate position requires nothing more than treating yourself patiently and compassionately in response to these painful feelings and moments.

Let's be clear here. You do not deny these wounded feelings, nor you deny that they are painful. You are simply responding to them in a different way.

Serving You Rather than Your Wounded Feelings

You are adopting a different "position." You're taking a step back and acknowledging that, as natural as these wounded feelings seem, they are in fact, simply that, wounded feelings. They are feelings being generated by a wounded place. They are not actually giving you accurate information about your worthiness. They are simply alerting you to hurt that wounded place.

In response to that hurt place, you choose first and foremost to be gentle, understanding and healing toward yourself.

Again, note the distinction; instead of collapsing and believing these false, self-negating feelings and treating yourself as a rotten person, and pushing yourself even harder. Choose to treat yourself with respect, care, and compassion. Give yourself affirmations that empower you. Apply kindness and understanding. These painful signals require positive affirmations. I do it often, and it works.

Remember, restoring your self-esteem is not about "fixing" yourself. It is about "feeding" yourself. Your job is not to address the underlying wound but to nourish the deprived, judged place from the root.

You do this by moving to this place not with harshness, but with patience and compassion.

In fact, that urgency and harshness to fix yourself is a symptom of your wounded self-esteem. This harsh approach to yourself is a repetition of the wounding and rejecting behavior.

When you choose to treat yourself calmly and compassionately, you're actually breaking that pattern of self-harshness. When you can step back and begin to be patient and accepting of yourself, despite what you "think" is wrong with you, that real sense of you begins to be nourished.

It wakes up. As you continue this approach, your healthy sense of self grows stronger and more durable. Just to be clear, self-acceptance does not preclude you from taking positive action for your growth and advancement or even making necessary changes in your life. In fact, these efforts'require you to be especially supportive, patient and approving towards yourself.

This is the very fuel you need to heal, make changes, and advance.

A Prescription for those Painful Moments of Self-Rejection

Needless to say, compassion and patience will probably not be your initial impulse when the feeling of worthlessness first rears its ugly head. Again, initially we'll want to collapse into these painful emotions.

When this happens, we need to pull ourselves back just a bit and remember that these are not accurate feelings. These are wounded feelings directing you to a wounded place. Let the discomfort remind you to be gentle and healing to yourself.

Consider it a prescription for these difficult moments. The more reactive and painful these places are, the more compassionate, gentle and patient you need to be with yourself.

CHAPTER 3

ACCEPTING YOURSELF JUST AS YOU ARE

O ne of the greatest needs a human being has is to be accepted for who they are. While this is the case, it doesn't necessarily mean that one can fulfill this need or that they believe it is even possible for them to accomplish it.

If people were generally encouraged to be themselves it would be easier for them to know that they can be accepted for who they are. What can make it so challenging is that there is a lot of pressure on people to be who other people want them to be.

If they become someone else, then this could be who their friends, family or society want them to be and then they would be accepted. It can then take a lot of strength for someone to be who they are and to resist the pressure and temptation to be who other people want them to be.

When It Does Exist

The pressure for a person to become someone else will come from people who do not accept themselves. Whenever someone accepts whom they are, they do not need to change others.

They can accept another person for whom they are. If not, then, they are likely to walk away. A person does not need to change just because people do not accept them.

Although people are different, they have a right to live a life that reflects who they are. That right should be respected—this is surely the right thing to do as long as they are not harming anyone else.

Self Acceptance

Just as there is so much pressure for one to be someone else, it is going to be important for one to accept themself. At times other people may accept them and other times they may not. If one has the need for everyone to accept them, they are going to suffer in more ways than one.

 When we accept ourselves, we are not going to need approval from everyone. We will be happy with who we are, meaning that other people's opinions are secondary.

Inner Strength

When one doesn't accept themself, there is the chance that the opinions of others are going to be primary and the opinion of himself/herself is going to be secondary. This does not mean that one should completely closed to receiving feedback just because they accept themselves.

What it means is that one is not going to allow other people to define whether they like themselves or not. This is therefore going to mean that one has more control over how they feel.

When I was a pastor, I struggled so much with being accepted. The opinions of others consistently warped my mind. I finally came to a place where I had to believe that I would never meet the demands or expectations of others. No matter what. I needed to get rid of the need to be accepted and appreciated by others. I needed self-acceptance. I needed to believe in my heart that I was just suitable for God. That was all that mattered. When I arrived at that place of self-acceptance, much weight was lifted from my shoulders. I finally accepted myself, thus, rendering me free.

Wide Open

When one doesn't accept themselves, they are likely to be wide open. They have no control over what they let in from others. Other people are then going to define who they are. They will have very little control over how they feel. If you are around people who accept you, everything will be fine. It is essential to surround yourself with people who have your best interests at heart and who celebrate you. There were times when I felt trapped. I did not know the actual role or purpose of some of the people I was around. I was wide open to their ideas of what they thought and what I should be or should not be. My suggestion to you is to take back your control.

False Self

A false self can cause someone to play a role and to do things that don't match up with his/her true needs and wants. That person is out of touch with whom they are, but the pay off is that other people will accept them. It is called people-pleasing.

A Common Approach

There is the chance that a person will hear that they should let go of the need for approval and they just need to 'accept' themselves. While this advice can assist someone, it can also make them close up. When this happens, one can end up denying the need to be accepted and as a result, they could end up feeling guilty or weak. Ignoring or repressing the need may work for some people. But it is not going to work for everyone.

A DeeperLook

The reason that people do not accept themselves and look to everyone else to accept them could be because no one has accepted them for who they are. Many who accept themselves could be the result of acceptance that they received from someone at an early point in their life. The person who received them or showed acceptance could have been a primary caregiver, loved one, etc. Furthermore, through their unconditional acceptance, one was able to realize that they are acceptable for who they are. If this did not take place during their childhood, someone else might have provided it.

Unconditional Acceptance

People are not likely going to look to others for approval once they have experienced unconditional acceptance. It is during the early stages of life that being accepted is matter of survival. Through being accepted,they are then able to grow out of this need.

If a person is never accepted for who they are, it is only natural that they are still going to look for what they did not receive all those years ago. Based on this outlook, this need not something that one need to remove, it is a need that one needs to fulfill. To what extreme will one be willing to go to satisfy that need? The answer is far. Until we become willing to accept ourselves, we will always be in search of unfulfilled fulfillment.

Awareness

Through being surrounded by people who accept you for who you are, it allows the undeveloped part of yourself to gradually develop. Once this happen, your emotional development will match up with your intellectual development.

This unconditional acceptance can be provided by a spiritual leader, therapist, or someone that can influence your life for the good. The qualifications they have or the method they may use is not important. What matters most is that they can offer the acceptance that is needed to grow.

CHAPTER 4

TRUST THE TRANSITION
DURING TIMES OF CHANGE

Change is a part of life, particularly if you have chosen to be on a path of spiritual growth. Even for those of us on this challenging yet rewarding path, change is not always as easy as we would like it to be. If you are faced with a more complicated change in your life right now, this book will help you remember to Trust Your Transition. It will also encourage you to trust life despite the outward appearances and the fearful pictures that can come to mind at a time like this.

Choosing to be on a path of spiritual growth usually involves taking responsibility for your part in your life. You are the co-creator of your life. This is where trust comes into play and where change can become a joyful experience.

I am sure that you chose to create a new, more joyful, and fulfilling reality at some point on your path.

Let me help to illustrate what it means to trust your transition. Let's say your plan is more extensive than what you have been experiencing as reality until now. There's a significant CHANGE. You have to go from where you are and how you feel now to where you are going and how you will feel when you live in that new reality.

God, our Creator, sees the best possible, most fulfilling, and pleasing outcome for you. Suddenly things begin to line up, and your mindset starts to change.

You have new intentions, and you begin to do your part in helping them to manifest. You saw yourself there, and you started to take the time to focus on the new life that you were creating. You are in your co-creative process. There is nothing to stop you now, but what is not seen is the other side of the co-creative process. You do not see all the fantastic things that God allows to happen behind the scenes.

Your renewed mindset and intention created a preferred direction for your life. It aligned with the will of God. The manifestation was something that words could not explain.

God, the All-Powerful organizing force behind creation, begins to orchestrate the fulfillment of your desire. God has already set up the potentials of all that needs to take place for it to become your reality.

God has set up all of the people that you need to meet, the book you need to read, and the words you need to hear being spoken to you. God perfectly orchestrates the inner transformation that needs to happen behind the scenes. This is an incredible process that we only get to see glimpses of now and then as our desires manifest into physical reality. As you continue to do your part, a lot is happening behind the scenes. God has sealed your destiny already. You must trust the transition to get to it and see it come to pass.

If you are wondering what does this have to do with change and trust, imagine that you have been focusing on manifesting your desire for some time and God has been naturally doing His part in this process. God orchestrated it to the point where you start to see things happening in your life. Your once stable foundation appears to dissolve right in front of you and suddenly situations begin to turn upside down. The natural response is fear. We say, "Oh, no, things cannot be spinning out of control like this! What's happening to me and why? "

This is where our trust comes in. Do you remember that great, new intention you set? This is how God begins shifting and changing what needs to change for your intention to be your reality. Here is an example, let's say you intend to find a new job that pays enough money to buy a house. You get the job and get settled there. After some years, you bought the home you wanted, but you get fired. Does these mean bad things are happening, and nothing is going, right? No! It means you needed to leave your job in order to create this new intention.

God always gives us exactly what we need. It is only us that forget that part about God. We get into fear mode, which is not necessary. In 2007, I had a contracting position with an excellent salary. I loved the money but hated the job. The money helped me to do many things. I was also a tad bit cocky in my attitude. Although I was ministering, I still felt like it was something missing. I wanted to do more with my life but, I could not quite figure it out.

Nevertheless, I was let go of that good-paying job. I never got fired a day in my life. Shortly after that, I fell. I went from a wheelchair to a walker and then a cane. I felt miserable. I had to wait until someone came home to change me and bathe me. I hated that vulnerable feeling. At that time, I couldn't see that all of this would work for my good. I was angry. As time passed, I had the chance to finish my projects. What and who I am today is the direct result of God allowing me to be fired and disabled so that He could bless me in due season.

If you find yourself in a time of immense change, look back and see what you have been focusing on manifesting. How might this change you are going through be bringing you closer to it? Are you willing to surrender control and trust your transition? Can you surrender your life to the wisdom of God?

Remember that God is in charge of the "how." The significant, crazy changes that can happen are all part of the Power of God moving forward with the "how." You know what? You most likely would not have chosen this "how" with your logical mind. You may say, "I would have done this or that." On this path, I have learned that everything God has ever given me has been more fulfilling and joyful than the "how" I would have picked to match my desire.

Why not trust? We must trust that the divine power of God is wisdom. God sees the bigger picture of your life. God is working for you, and you have to trust and understand that when you start to see some crazy things happening in your life and change is knocking at your door, you will know what's going on. The energy that you have been dreaming of, you are now being taken to it. You must remember that it is your job to be willing to take the actions you are being called to take. Keep in mind that you actually created this and that is a good thing. Maybe you did not create the "how," but you chose the desire of your heart. God lovingly and carefully has created the "how" in front of you for you to take. It is time for you to be free from the bondage of doubt and begin to trust. Allow yourself to believe, especially on this path of spiritual growth while creating your most fulfilling life. Resisting will only cause pain and unnecessary stress.

In my moments of uncertainty, I often found myself in dark places. The bondage of doubt had clouded both my judgment and my ability to make sound decisions that I intuitively knew were for my betterment. I had to reconnect to my Higher Power (God). I did this not by talking but by allowing myself to believe. I asked God to restore in me the faith and trust that I once had. Slowly, I began to see myself in a different place emotionally and spiritually. I reminded myself that I wanted something more. I was failing at doing my part. Therefore, I had to get a renewed level of trust.

When in doubt, trust God. I know that you cannot see it all right now. You may not see the big picture, but God knows your beginning from your end. These times of change can be truly joyful and ease filled when you trust God during this significant transition.

CHAPTER 5

FIND A PEACEFUL PLACE

M any people are looking for peace and are looking in the wrong places. They are looking outside of themselves to find it.

We need contrast to experience our physical reality and to be human. Contrast is experienced here in the duality of living on earth. It is experienced in the positive and the negative, the good and the bad and the yin and the yang.

The problem is not with the duality. It is our judgment of it that creates the problems and create our suffering.

It's All Good – Even When It's Bad

The "bad" is nothing more than framework for the "good." One could not know and experience the good without experiencing the bad. Likewise, joy cannot be tasted without sensing and knowing what makes you sad. It is like the four seasons, each time and event has it's place under the sun.

If you are experiencing undue hardship right now, and you find the silver lining in the dark cloud, give thanks for that. That cloud can begin to lift for you. You may be able to experience a flash of sunlight as a reminder to let you know that the sunlight is still there. It is always daytime somewhere on the earth.

Like the tides of the sea, there are moments in our life when things are low. They are ebbing out to sea and all seems lost. Like breathing and the space between breaths, there is this point where the tide is neither rising nor falling, and it is here where you must find your peace.

The Place Between Places is Where You Find Peace

This place between places is the center of the Vortex, the center of the eye of the hurricane where all is peaceful and calm. To get to that center, you must go within—there is no other answer. Seeking, the answer outside of you, will throw you into the hurricane and toss you about like a rag doll. I know firsthand about going outside to fix an inside issue. That is why it is essential to chase peace. When catastrophes begin to happen, and global events occur that send others reeling, when you know and live in your center, nothing can ultimately disturb you from that place of peace, except for you.

Sometimes, we are the cause of our own suffering. We suffer because we continue to judge what is good and bad in our lives. When you let go of the judgment, you can let go of the suffering. You will come to the hidden valley where the brooks babble happily in their meandering to the ocean. The birds chirp merrily in their dance in between trees. You hear the lazy sounds of bumblebees busying themselves with their business. This serves to let you know that all is truly well. God forgives and forgets, but we hold on and judge ourselves harshly. Once again, stuck in bondage.

All is truly well

I know how hard life can be at times. There may be periods of uncertainty and confusion. But that is if you keep your eyes focused on the events and circumstances that are going on outside of you. You may be wondering How To Find Peace in this crazy world. Know that you get it by looking outside of yourself -- God dwells within. All things work together for our good. We have to believe it.

That's the mistake most people make. They take "God" out of everything that they judge. If you judge and focus on the negative, you will surely wreak negative havoc in your life. To find peace, place your focus on those things that bring you joy and thankfulness –this will always work and force you within.

3 Practices to Stay Strong

1. *Acceptance*. We get so busy trying to change people, places and things that we never allow ourselves the pleasure of just being. Not accepting things as they are is a declaration that this moment is "wrong," we assume that certain feelings or situations are "bad" and left unchanged, we will be unacceptable. Why?   Because that's what we learned as

children and no one teaches us to "question" the validity of our assumptions and beliefs. Acceptance does not mean lying down as a floor mat for the dirty shoes of the world. It means bringing your awareness into the situation, recognizing what contributions you have made for events to appear as they are and then determining what actions to take to rectify the situation. Non-acceptance is the resistance to what already is, and trying to change what already is, is futile and frustrating - as the saying goes "what your resist, persists." Free up your energy and reclaim your power by allowing the moment to be as it is – then work towards making the changes that you desire.

2. *Let go of the need to always having to be correct.* Let go of the need to always having to be right. A Course in Miracles asks the question "Would you rather be right, or happy?" A question that seems simple, yet one that many people have to ponder over! We've all been in the situation of being in an argument, only to realize we can't remember what it was about. Still, we'll persist in our viewpoint simply for the sake of being right. What makes you do you think you're right anyhow? You have one viewpoint. A single perspective that cannot possibly encompass all that has gone on to create this moment. If you're "right" then you would have to know the "truth," but what "truth" do you refer to? For the truth to be accurate, it has to apply equally to all people, in all situations

with no variations. If one person is right and the other wrong, how can this be the "truth" on which to base being right? Being right is sometimes a tool to feel righteous or superior to cover issues of low confidence, lack of self-esteem etc. Instead of trying to prop up the illusion of being superior, decide to be happy by accepting that others have different opinions and perceptions and all can be tolerated, including ours.

3. *Practice non-judgement*. No one enjoys being judged. Yet it's a habit that we engage in constantly by assessing, comparing and valuing ourselves and others. We're all experts in how others should live their lives; how they should dress, what entertainment they should enjoy, how their kids should behave etc. without having the relevant qualifications to judge. Similar to being right, judgement is a sucker's game that draws us in and leaves us with feelings of being separated, alone and isolated. Differing opinions and beliefs are part of our human make up. The contrast they provide gives us variety and diversity, making our lives richer and more exciting .Practicing non-judgment is an excellent portal to learning about ourselves.

The first step to non-judgment is awareness. By placing your awareness on your thoughts and feelings, you'll quickly recognize when you've slipped into judgment mode by the critical nature of your thoughts. Once you have become aware of your thoughts, you can then begin to question their validity or truth.   Quite often you'll find that perhaps you were mistaken, inaccurate or your judgement was uninformed and half-baked.   Once you're aware of your thoughts and their limitations, your awareness will begin to dissolve the judgments and silence the inner critic running amok in your mind.

CHAPTER 6

OVERCOME FEAR AND IMPROVE CONFIDENCE

Overcoming fear is one of the greatest challenges that you will face as you learn how to improve your self-esteem and self-confidence to become free.

Imagine that you lived in the 17th century when there were no airplanes and parachutes. Imagine you lived happily with your family at the top of the mountain until you ran out of food and water. You can see all the water and the food that you need to help your family survive from the top. However, to reach the water and food you need to overcome your fear and jump. You know that when you jump you will dive into the river beneath the mountain and not suffer physical injury. You also know that it will change your life to jump because you will be able to gather all the food and water your family needs. But first, you must overcome the fear and doubt that is holding your back. You also need to overcome questions triggered by fear on your mind and max you anxious, "what if i hit the rock?" "What if I can't find a ways to climb back up?" 'What if..." Our lives are not too different from this story. We sometimes face difficulties and challenges such as being unhappy at work, not satisfied with our bodies because we picked up weight, toxic relationships and criticism. This results in us being unfulfilled. From this we also experience low self-esteem and a lack of confidence. We know that if we could just take a leap of faith and jump to change our lives. It would improve, but, we remain scared of jumping. Fear and anxiety holds us back. Doubt cripples our attempts.

Overcoming fear is one of the most important skills that you need to learn in your life in order to get unstuck and take your life forward. Fear affects decision making and a lack of decision making power causes poor results. At times, because of fear and doubt, one may not take the action needed to change their life.

Fear can manifest itself in many ways. It can also affect you in serious life decisions and stop you from taking action to succeed --whether its starting a new business or quitting the job that does not help you become fulfilled.

Here are 5 ways that you can use to overcome fear in your life and get unstuck.

1. *Realize that fear is not something given to us by God* - Often when we experience fear, we focus more on trying to eliminate it than trying to face it. People that succeed face the same fears as we face but they act despite their fears. Their process,

unlike some of us, does not focus on eliminating the fear, but focuses on managing the fear. God did not intend for us to be fearful. In the face of fear, we can remind ourselves of times when we did not allow fear to control us.

2. *Realize that fear can be both rational and irrational*- As people we have an internal conversation also known as self-talk. The little voice inside our head sometimes gives us messages that causes us to have doubt....then we begin to question ourselves - "maybe I shouldn't," "maybe now is not the right time," "what if this and what if that"...instead of acting, we then leave the status quo and do nothing. Our lives don't change and we remain unhappy for years. Only to look back into our lives many years later and have regrets. You must improve your level of awareness regarding self-talk. The minute your internal voice tells you to doubt... stop and question yourself. Here are few questions you need to ask yourself and overcome irrational fear, "What am I really afraid of? What's the worst thing that can happen? Am I realistic or is fear ruling me?"

3. *Define your fear* - Don't let fear get irrational. Define what it is that you are afraid of. If you were to quit your job, what would you be afraid of? Is it the fact that you won't find another job or is it just the imaginative discomfort of finding a new job? What about a new business, why would you be afraid to start? So what if you fail perhaps go broke... maybe you can

get back to working. Define the fear. Once you define the fear, you are in a better position to take the next step.

4. *Make an action plan to manage your fear or just accept it* - List your fears and make an action plan to resolve them.

 If you want to start a business and you are worried you will lose money then make a plan to absorb the risk. Maybe you can have funds allocated in case you lose money or diversify your investment in some way.

If what you feel is just irrational fear (which might feel very real) as opposed to rational fear, you must accept the discomfort and act despite the fear. Make a contingency in your planning for the practical things that you are worried about and accept any emotional discomfort that you might experience so that you are better able to act no matter what. This will help you improve your confidence.

5. *Take action and learn more about yourself*- Often when we feel fear, we make problems much bigger than what they actually are. We also forget that sometimes lifes decisions are about learning and improving as we might not always get things right, at first time. So take action on your endeavours and be willing to have a learning attitude. Doing this will help you overcome fear and improve your self-confidence.

CHAPTER 7

TRIUMPHING OVER TOUGH TIMES

Right now many people are facing tough times. Life as we once knew it has changed .We may find ourselves confronting situations that we have never dealt with before. While we might not be able to control things that are occurring in the world, we can control how we react to what is happening. Specifically, we can control how we use our minds and thoughts to get through difficult circumstances. The following are simple steps that will not only help you handle any challenges, but will allow you to move through them to achieve success.

1. *Remember, this too shall pass* - Sometimes when we are faced with tough times we feel as if they will never end. We can't see the "light at the end of the tunnel" to that time when our problems are resolved. It seems as if we will always have to deal with the difficulty. This can be a very negative attitude to adopt because it leads to a sense of hopelessness – why bother trying to change things because it won't make a difference anyway? Now is the time to remember that, as with

most things in life, this too shall pass. You will find another job, business will pick up, the pain and grief will subside. As you realize that this challenging time will be replaced by a brighter tomorrow. You will find it easier to take the necessary steps to resolve your situation.

2. *Consider past successes-* Often when we are dealing with a problematic situation, we develop amnesia about our past. Unless you are one of a privileged few, you have successfully overcome prior challenges in your life. Think about past events when you've been tougher than your problems. It will help you realize deep within. You have the strength and fortitude to move beyond this demanding time.

3. *Determine your personal success strategy-* As you recall those times when you've triumphed over trouble, consider what strategies you used to accomplish it. Each of us has many successful strategies that we've used in our past. However, we often forget to pullout those strategies during those times when we can most benefit from them. Determine what worked for you before and apply those successful ideas now. You will find it much easier to handle any adversity you may be facing.

4. *Handle day-to-day challenges,* but envision your goal – When we go through difficult times, it is easy to get bogged down in the minutiae of the situation and forget where we are headed. Take timeout to envision what life will be like when the

situation has reached a successful outcome. Handle the day-to-day details such as making follow-up phone calls, finding new ways to market yourself or your business and solving daily problems. Always remind yourself of how things will look and feel when you are triumphant. This will provide you with the motivation to continue taking action and it will also help you maintain a positive attitude.

5. *Find a support system-* When we are struggling with major challenges it is very difficult to consistently stay upbeat. We don't get the position, we lose the sale. The expenses continue to pile up as the money gives out. This is the time when we need others to help us remain focused and optimistic. Call a confidante who can see the bright side when you can't. Talk to a trusted friend who will help you leave your 'pity party' and take action once again.   There are times when even the strongest and most positive of us need others to help us navigate through the trials of trouble. My circle is very small but it's a safe circle. I can call them at any time along with my spiritual dad, who always make it a point to help me to see the bigger picture.

6. *Focus on what is right in your life-* When we are confronted by problems, it is very easy to let them control your perspective on life. We spend too much time and energy focusing on what is wrong and very little time thinking about what is right. On a daily basis, come up with a list of things that

are good in your life, things for which you can be grateful even as you travel this tough road. It will help you realize that even though the world may seem to be falling apart around you, you still have many positives in your life.

CHAPTER 8

PRESS UNDER PRESSURE

D o you ever feel like you simply can't deal with all of the pressure that is placed on you on a daily basis? Are you being pressured to complete many different tasks at the same time? Are you having a hard time getting anything done because the pressure is like the weight of the world on your shoulders?

We have all been in situations like this and, instead of letting the pressure get the best of you, you need to choose positivity. No matter what circumstances arise, we must press on despite it all. We must not allow the pressures of life to consume us. You can stay positive and combat it with what I call "pressure affirmations."

Staying Positive When You are Under Pressure

What are Pressure Affirmations?

"Pressure affirmations" are positive statements that will help you get through high pressure or intense situations more easily. Sometimes you just need a little help believing in yourself and believing that you can get done what needs to get done. Other times, you need to choose a positive attitude so you can deal with the people around you who are stressing you out.

Pressure affirmations are things that you can easily make a part of your daily life so that you are able to control those high pressure situations without letting your emotions get the best of you.

Transform Negative Energy into Positive Power

When you make use of pressure affirmations, you will find that you can take the negative power out of these situations and turn it into power that you can use to push yourself. When you break down situations in this way, you will find that you can use the wasted energy (spent worrying) for good. You will likely be able to get through high pressure situations much easier. Pressure affirmations help you look at your life and the situations that you encounter in a more positive light.

You may not realize it, but having pressure placed on you is actually a good thing and when you begin using pressure affirmations, you will see this for yourself. If you didn't feel pressured to get something done, you likely won't even bother trying. In fact, you may not even set your alarm so you could get up in the morning and get things done.

CHAPTER 9

LONELY BUT NOT ALONE

———————✳———————

Loneliness is a tricky thing to combat. Loneliness seems to beget loneliness. When you feel isolated you crawl into your shell and become more so. You feel separated from other human beings. You may have physical symptoms too, like an ache or a heaviness in your chest. It's not a good feeling.

Trying to combat loneliness is not an option. One must take it in and fully own it. Pay attention to how you feel. Be aware of your body. Let yourself be sad and acknowledge the sorrow. Give yourself permission to cry. It's important to be aware of your feelings before you can take steps to heal.

Sometimes people try to distract themselves from their loneliness with alcohol, the internet, busyness, shopping and more. Distraction devices are limitless. You can stave off your feelings by plunging into chores or playing video games or whatever keeps you occupied. I know how to busy myself, and what I discovered is that I did not want to feel.

Some people try to explain their loneliness by cataloging all their faults. Of course, they are unworthy of others. Who would want to be with them when they are so flaw-ridden and undesirable? This kind of dangerous thinking offers them an explanation, but it's a false one.

Loneliness is part of the human condition

You may be lonely, but you're not alone. At one time or another, most people have felt lonely. And if you encountered a lonely person, you would show compassion to him/her. You would not blame them for their condition. You would give them support.

The same applies to you. When you're feeling lonely, try to have compassion for yourself. Understand that you may be feeling this way for a reason. Perhaps, your connections with friends and family, have frayed a bit. Perhaps your relationships are not as close as you would wish. Loneliness is a kind of emotional pain that signals-like a physical pain-that something in your body needs attention. In this case, that something is your connection to God. When your relationship with God grows, you will soon discover that you were never alone.

Are You Lonely or Just Alone?

Being alone doesn't necessarily mean loneliness. Many people enjoy the calmness and clarity of being alone for relatively long periods of time; rather than being involved in the often chaotic dramas of other people's lives.

A sense of loneliness can be something we have become accustomed to from a very early age. Having parents/care-givers who were not emotionally available and attuned to you; or being amongst siblings and family members who were noticeably 'different' to you, induces a sense of semi-isolation, of being there, but not really being there; of 'going through the motions' in our dealings with others and of being lonely in a crowd. Lastly, amongst others, yet still solitary.

Some of us had a less-than-good-enough childhood, and formed few attachments with people because the people around us were neglectful, unreliable or threatening. We may have, instead, formed attachments to animals, objects, hobbies, or perhaps to our own ideas, wishes and dreams.

To have an 'Attachment Disorder' can condemn us to a life without meaningful and rewarding relationships. As we mature, we can slowly learn to build trust in a stable and reliable person and take the risk of making an emotional attachment - with its inherent threat of loss and pain, which we know we can survive if need to be.

Some people will have a self-imposed loneliness because they have, in the past, felt 'trapped' in relationships with their family and/or spouse/partner. They avoid getting close to other people as a way of ensuring they don't feel trapped and thwarted again. The obvious cost of this is to remain without the deeper intimate connection that most humans deeply desire.

Internet dating sites and chat rooms offer a relatively quick, easy and inexpensive way to make contact with other people; but they are not a salve for deeper loneliness. Indeed the disappointment and rejection often reported by users of such sites can only add to feelings of failure, alienation and isolation.

The 'commitment phobic' may deeply desire loving contact and to have some of their needs met by another; but they cannot take that step to an exclusive, reciprocal and emotionally intimate relationship. This may be because they only have experience of bad relationships. They may have a core-belief that they don't deserve to be in a good relationship. They may have felt 'engulfed' in a previous relationship and lost their own identity; or they may have been over-burdened with responsibilities in their past; and they fear that this will happen again. Many a partner of such a person has only found this out after years of hoping, waiting, wishing and broken promises.

Some of us ensure that our lives are very busy. we are in demand, and are having a 'full life'. This can be just a sham, as we attempt to fully occupy our time and distract us from a deeper gnawing sense of loneliness. Distraction activities such as over-working and over-socializing are ways to avoid the intensity of the pain of alone-ness. Having lots of superficial 'friends' can be a way of avoiding deeper intimacy and can also lead to feeling lonely, even though we have a network of 'contacts' - particularly in this 'social media' age. One deeper intimate relationship is more beneficial to our soul than a large number of acquaintances could ever be.

We have to wrestle with the difference between our human and spiritual awareness and needs.

We all like to think that we are 'masters of our own ship' and 'charting our own course' .But whether we are a lone sailor traversing the world's oceans, or part of a team/crew can only be our choice – despite the needs or hopes of others. We may have to go beyond our deeper fear and take the risk of connecting and relating with others, and travelling as part of a team albeit, perhaps, a small team.

We all need to balance time alone spent in reflection and planning, with time spent with others; sharing ourselves with them at different levels.

Don't allow loneliness to push you into bad relationships or 'friendships.' You may feel lonely, but you can still be discerning about who you want to spend your time with, and what will enrich your life.

The most crucial point is to develop an intimate relationship with our Creator. So many times, we want to blame God for our hardships. That is further from the truth. Building spiritual intimacy grants us the balance needed during periods of solitude.

CHAPTER 10

PURSUE YOUR PURPOSE IN LIFE

Everybody longs for a purpose in this life. Philosophers have brainstormed on the meaning of life and have arrived at different answers. Good people love to do good deeds and help others in need. Even seemingly evil people know how to achieve their purpose. In some cases, people believe that having a negative purpose is better than having none at all. If you do not know your purpose, you are simply breathing in and breathing out. Existence. That is all you ever have. You do not have a meaningful life. Living is way different from existing!

In pursuing your purpose, you need to determine where your passions lie. In doing so, you can know where to focus your energies and not waste time trying to do and achieve everything all at once. Life is too short to achieve everything, not to mention, it is physically impossible to achieve every single thing that you put your mind to. This is why you need to rediscover your passions since these will point you to your purpose.

Go back to your childhood dreams. Although much has changed since your childhood days, your dreams are still there buried somewhere inside your heart. There may be a lot of things that have covered it. Nevertheless, if you genuinely engage yourself in digging more deeply in your heart, you will find that those dreams are still intact even if they have transformed through the years. Write the names of the people you admire.

The people you admire and treat as role models also play an important role for you to rediscover your passions. Although these people may be very different from who you are, they have qualities and traits that are mirrored in you. After all, the people that you would come to admire are people who share some traits with you.

Understand what your skills and talents are. Your education through the classroom, through the books that you have read, and the experiences you went through molded you into who you are now. Along the way, you have also picked up skills and talents that help you deal with the things that you want to do and accomplish. By taking note of these skills and talents, you are creating an inventory of tools that you will bring with you on the journey to your purpose.

Five Mistakes That Keep You From Finding Your Purpose

As humans, we want to have some kind of purpose in life- an answer to the question "why" that keeps us going. However, for some of us, finding this purpose is not easy. Sometimes, it's not clear as to what we are meant to do with our life. If you feel that you are stuck and are unsure as what to do, you may be doing something that is hindering you from figuring things out. Here are five of those things that could possibly be making it difficult for you to find your purpose.

1. *You don't set aside time to reflect on your purpose--* The fast paced lifestyle that we have today is often not conducive for reflection. When was the last time we actually set aside time to just pray and reflect on who we are and what we want to do with our life? It's important that we set aside some time to actually think things through and figure things out. Sometimes, it is during reflection time that allows us to clear our minds and focus on what we really want to do.

2. *You don't pay attention to your feelings--* While we ought to think logically about our purpose in life, sometimes we also forget about our feelings-what our gut instincts tell us. The Christian faith tells us that God can also speak to us through our feelings. If you are doing something and you have feelings of dissatisfaction and restlessness, pay attention-that might be

God's way of telling you that there are greater things ahead or in store for you.

3. *You let your friends or family decide for you--* Sometimes it can be terribly difficult to make decisions and we can be very indecisive. Because of this, it can be tempting to simply go with what our friends and family think. Many people often take on a certain profession or goal in life because that was expected from them. While this may be good, it can also sometimes lead to us stagnating and settling, when in truth we could go on and do things that we are truly passionate about.

4. *You are afraid to make mistakes or to change--* I remember calling my spiritual dad while I was on the side of the road. I was panicking and crying. When he asked what the problem was. My response was, "I am afraid I'm going to mess up." I was in a place that I have never been in before, and the newness of it overwhelmed me.

Often, we want to be able to get it right the first time. We don't allow ourselves to make mistakes. It is important to be open to change and to pick ourselves up if we have made a decision that does not seem to be entirely right. Especially if we have discerned our passion, and find that we are wrong or are being led to somewhere else due to new information or new needs..

5. *You want to be sure ALL the time--* Lastly, people usually want certainty. This is normal, and of course we want to be

sure before committing to something, in order to make sure we can stick by it through thick or thin. However, we also need to realize that our purpose will still have some uncertainty in terms of the details, how it will pan out, and where it will lead you. Always remember that despite the risks and uncertainty, God is with you every step of the way, and that your purpose, while there will be many twists and turns along the way, will always bring something worth while that will leave you with a certain peace and joy that comes with finding who you are and what you are meant to do.

CHAPTER 11

OVERCOMING DISTRACTIONS

Distractions are often things in our surroundings that capture our attention frequently, even if they have absolutely no connection to what we're presently doing.

Sometimes, it's our own fault that we are distracted. You check your Facebook, IG or Twitter when you get bored while at work. You open your email even if you just checked it a few minutes ago and you check your phone for text messages.

Sometimes, the distractions come from other people who are not fully aware of your need to finish your own tasks and obligations..

There will also be situations where other people end up wasting your time in trivial matters, simply because you are available at that time. Interactions can easily turn into full-blown distractions that take you away from your work, leading to delays and toxic levels of stress.

How can you effectively manage electronic distractions like emails, instant messages, etc.?

We are already living (and entirely immersed) in the age of electronics. At the present time, people have to contend not only with email, but they also have to deal with conventional phone calls, Skype, instant messages, texts, FaceTime and the list goes on and on.

A person can be as connected as they wish to other people. But as an immediate drawback, they would have to tend all active communication channels. In the beginning, it may seem fun to have so many ways to talk to family, friends and co-workers. However, the novelty wears off very quickly when you're in the middle of a tough working day .Your smartphone's notifications are going off every 5-10 minutes. Here are some ways that you can manage this type of distraction::

1. *Check & Answer in Batches* - Don't look at every email and text message as soon as you receive them, especially if you have to finish something urgent.

 Acknowledge that you have received them and check the mail later. If you check each message individually as they arrive, you are going to get very distracted and you may lose the vital momentum that you may have had. I had to learn how to turn my phone off or put it on silent.

2. *Turn Off Instant Notifications* - Today's devices are extremely efficient in notifying users when new emails, IMs or text messages are received. However, this efficiency doesn't really support the type of productivity that you need to finish critical and time-sensitive tasks.

As I said in the previous step, I had to put my phone on silent. Put your phone or computer on "silent mode" and focus on finishing your tasks. Again, you can check all your new messages at a later time, after you've made some progress in your work..

3. *Respond with Short Messages* - Don't call someone unless it's absolutely necessary to do so. Of course, this guideline doesn't apply to family members. Call your spouse or children the moment something important or urgent comes up.

How can you prevent visitors from distracting you?

There will be times when visitors are just not welcomed anymore because of the large number of tasks you have to finish very soon. Visitors are distractions, plain and simple. If you can't afford to stay around anymore, it's best to manage the amount of time you give other people.

Here are some tips to prevent visitors from robbing you of precious working time:

1. *Let Them Know* – This is the most effective way to persuade a visitor to leave. Simply let the them know that you are unavailable because you have to finish something an urgent and important task.

Tell the visitor that you will contact him/her at a later time, after you're done with what you're doing. However, I would dissuade you from saying this to everyone who visits as you may end up with a long list of "I'll get back to you's" at the end of the day.

2. *Change Your Location*-If you're doing something at home, avoid high traffic areas. I call this "hiding" because you're removing yourself from people's line of sight. Out of sight, out of mind! Changing your working spot may give you a temporary reprieve from distractions.

3. *Don't Be Available* - If you allow people to distract you, they will, simply because they can. If you have a chair near your desk, put something on it so people won't be tempted to sit down for a "quick chat." Put on some headphones, so people won't be tempted to make small talk.

These tips are mere to keep you focused and not allow your time to be monopolized by others.

CHAPTER 12

WHEN IT SEEMS LIKE ITS OVER

When you feel overwhelmed by life, rather than focusing on finding a different set of more manageable problems (as if that were even possible), you should look for ways to raise your life-condition so you can gain access to the wisdom, courage, and energy that you need to solve the problems that you have. If you do not have a process or a practice that does this for you, then find one. Willpower and intellect alone is often insufficient.

This is the real answer about what to do when everything seems to be going wrong: find a way to transform your perspective so that obstacles become opportunities. If that seems too abstract, or you're having trouble finding a practice that works for you, or you're not interested in finding a practice at all, I'd like to offer the following techniques for making yourself feel better when you feel bad. These are just some comforting thoughts really--but ones that you might find useful.

TRICKS AND COMFORTING THOUGHTS THAT MAY WORK

1. *So a man thinketh, so he is*. Visualize yourself succeeding. As a professional skier envisions every twist and turn of a ski run before making it, imagine yourself on the other side of a problem. Even if the abstract can activate a powerful belief in your ability to succeed. Do it even though you have no idea how to win. A belief that you can-- even a "blind" faith can be empowering if it is a belief in yourself.

2. *Avoid making important life decisions when your life-condition is low*. The kind of thoughts that you'll have in general are always more reflective of your life-condition at the moment rather than the circumstances in which you find yourself. You'll best avoid future misery if you can consciously recognize when circumstances have gotten you down and thereby produced gloomy feelings and thoughts of defeat. Those "I Can" moments are nowhere to be found. Trust me; I've fallen into this situation too many times.

3. *Imagine you've already achieved* a desired goal (one you're completely confident you can) and celebrate now in the joy you anticipate you'll feel later. I've often found that daydreaming about future successes lifts my spirits by bouncing my mind out of my present difficulties into future imagined glories.

4. *Force yourself* to focus on one problem at a time. Focus on what's easiest, most important, or that which you can solve soonest. Reducing the total number of challenges confronting you will be an enormous relief and help combat the tendency to feel defeated when facing what seems to be an overwhelming number of problems.

5. *Wait.* My four favorite words for weathering all storms: **this too shall pass**. Think of entering into a waiting mode as an active process, not a passive acceptance of whatever fate has in store for you—other good things often happen that raise your life-condition and enable you to handle the mess you're facing more easily. You may think you know all the bad things that are going to happen, but outcomes we anticipate---good and bad---most often don't turn out the way we envisioned.

6. *Access your creativity to solve problems.* Reduce the chatter in your head by listening to moving music, praying, meditating, reading positive works, etc. Solutions often bubble up from the subconscious when the conscious mind floats.

7. *Find something positive to distract you.* Take a real break from thinking about your problems when you're not actively engaged in solving them. Because it's much harder to turn off obsessive thoughts about the challenges facing you than turn on more positive thoughts, finding something genuinely distracting is the best strategy. Humor works for me as long as

it's humor that's genuinely funny. Writing poetry, working on scripts and reading also works. There is nothing wrong with taking a break from fighting the good fight to recharge your batteries. In fact, strange as this may sound, there's nothing wrong with engaging in controlled denial. It can be an extremely effective way to combat anxiety, as long as you don't let it prevent you from acting when action is required.

8. *Take on your anxiety directly.* Identify the thoughts that make you anxious and follow them to their logical extreme. Wrap your mind around what it would feel like for your worst fears to be realized. What would you do then? Often if we force ourselves to imagine the worst in concrete terms it feels less frightening than it does when we imagine it abstractly..

9. *Ask for help.* You do not have to do it all by yourself. Many of us are independent in most areas of our lives, and when in an uncomfortable place, ask for help. You will be surprised at how many people will avail themselves to you. They want to see you on the other side. I remember being down and not knowing which way to turn, I called my friend, and she came over, sat with me, and let me vent. She made up my bed, ran my shower, and took my outfit out for me. We went out and had a great time.   If I had never opened my mouth to express my needs, I would've continued to struggle.

10. *Accept that you must face something unpleasant.* Stop worrying about experiencing pain and trying to avoid it. You'll make it through and survive. Prepare yourself to feel whatever there is to feel. The longer you wait to feel it, the more anticipatory dread you'll feel as well. As Nichiren Daishonin wrote, "Suffer what there is to suffer. Enjoy what there is to enjoy. Regard both suffering and joy as facts of life."

11. **Whatever you're going** through actually does represent an opportunity for growth. The thing about cliches is that they're mostly true.

12. *There will come a time when you'll struggle even to remember what's causing you so much anguish.* It's hard to project yourself into that future. Still, if you stop to think about it, you've almost certainly already forgotten about most of the trying experiences that you've faced in the past (not, of course, the life-changing experiences---but most things that get us down on a daily basis are much more mundane).

CHAPTER 13

STOPPING THE BLAME GAME

The blame game has no end. It is a circle that constantly feeds into itself. This game is one that we are all familiar with and have, no doubt, participated in the playing of it from time to time. The popular game starts when we are children by pointing fingers at one another, with cries of, "he did it, she did it, or they did it." The source of unraveling the misbehavior is usually left up to a responsible adult who is in charge and often the culprit is identified, and lessons for that incident are learned. We adults, smugly reason that it is part of the process that children face as they are growing up, and go merrily on our way.

However, it is pretty clear from the number of adults who play this game, that lessons are yet to be learned. Everyone agrees that we have had enough of this game from the politicians. We want solutions, not bickering, blaming and more finger pointing. We all know that leads to nowhere, a stalemate, and more of the same.

Because people, including those in leadership roles, do not want to take responsibility for their mistakes that cause grief of one sort or another to someone else, the blame game has taken on a life of its own. Whether we look at political campaigning, government policies, financial affairs, business activities, educational pursuits, religious organizations, the sports arena, international relationships or in our personal lives, there is always someone else to blame. It is almost like a virus that has permeated every face of our society.

So what about the rest of us? When we look in the mirror, do we see someone there who also plays this game? Most of us, if we are being honest with ourselves, would have to respond with a yes. The playing of this game occurs often during little encounters in our personal lives such as who left the lights on, to blaming the other guy as to why we got that traffic ticket, to bigger issues of blaming the fast foods restaurants (from whom we freely choose to eat by exercising our own free will) on our bad health.

One source to understand the sheer volume of those playing the blame game is the number of lawyers and judges, who are playing the roles of coaches and referees in the huge backlogged court system which is the playground for those who are serious participants in this game. While it is certainly true that there are a sufficient number of legitimate cases of outright neglect and criminal intent in the legal system, there is also a huge amount of cases that ferment and occupy this playing court simply because of the popular and insidious blame game.

There are many reasons that people participate in playing this game, but the most common reasons are:

1) Not wanting to be identified as making a mistake,
2) Not wanting others to know of our mistakes,
3) Not wanting to be punished, and the most important one is,
4) Not wanting to take responsibility for our mistakes.

All of this blaming does not resolve problems or bring about peaceful solutions. This is true for the smallest incidents on the playground to huge international controversies played out every single day in our world.

Playing this game of blaming someone else is not the answer for peace building. Taking responsibility and working together to resolve issues is the answer.

Picking Up the Pieces

What makes you a resilient individual is your ability to take the falls in your life and learn to pick up the pieces. This is not entirely an easy thing to do of course. It depends on how badly the adversities have hit you. The fact of the matter is, that life, perse', has a way of re-inventing itself if you give it a chance.

You may ask how. For starters, take a good look in the mirror and ask yourself – who am I?

The answer is, you are what you think you are. Remember that so a man thinketh, so he is. If you see a loser reflecting in the mirror, that is what you will become, a loser. However, if you were to visualize a person of great emotional and mental energy and try gravitating towards that perception you might see yourself in a more positive light.

Here are some insights on how you can learn to pick up the pieces:

Do not Avoid Problems that you Face

Problems are part of our lives. We cannot avoid it neither can we have an ultimate solution that can solve all problems. It is quite natural to avoid problems especially when you see yourself hitting rock bottom. However, if you start avoiding the problems that confronts you, it is not going to go away. It may even come back to you in a more difficult form.

What you can do is to see every problem that you face as a challenge that you need to resolve and move forward. This may not be an easy thing to do. Especially when you are confronted with those specific kinds of problems where there is no clear solution. Here is where you need to take a cold hard look to see what you can do about it. If you can set it aside and move on then perhaps that's what you've got to do. Otherwise, you need to keep looking harder to see what else you can do about it. Remember that problem solving is always a better option that problem avoidance. If logic fails to give you the kind of solutions that you seek, you may have to start thinking creatively.

Learn to Decide Quickly

As the saying goes life is short! So there are moments when you've got to make decisions quickly. There may be some decisions that you have to make that might put you in a moral and ethical dilemma. This is when you need to peg your decisions to values and principles. The question that you have to ask yourself is, " Am I doing things in the right way or should I do the right thing?" Ultimately this is a matter of choice. When you do the right thing, you will see yourself as a person of high integrity. This might not quite solve the dilemma that you are in, but it will give you the peace of mind that you hav not compromised on your values and principles.

Ride the Waves of Uncertainty

When crisis and hard time descends upon you, you feel yourself to be in uncharted and choppy waters. This is when you need to keep your bearings and stay the course that you intend to go no matter what. Keep telling yourself that you have the power of charting your own course and not to be swept away by the changes in circumstances. Sometimes you might find yourself in this situation because the kind of information that you have or are receiving is not entirely correct and are being influenced into a type of thinking that obviously is not working. This is when you need to take a cold hard look at what is going on. If there is a need to change your thinking and your actions, change it.

One day at a Time

When you are hit by tough time, take the challenges that you face one day at a time. There is an age old saying that states "it takes many droplets of water to make the mighty ocean." There are many issues in our lives that we cannot solve immediately. Some of these issues are recurrent and rears its ugly head from time to time. This is when you need to take things as they come. Create a 'one day at a time' kind of attitude. Learn to prioritize the issues that you face and tackle those that you can solve quickly and measurably. For bigger issues, break them into smaller pieces and tackle them one at a time. Keep a log of what you are doing so that you can measure your progress. Just keep at trying to solve the problems that you are facing and you will eventually find a workable solution.

CHAPTER 14

DARE TO DREAM

Life is not a rosy path. You should take all the necessary steps for succeeding in your endeavors. Some people may make attempts to succeed in life, but, due to lack of focus, they do not know the right steps to be taken. As a result, they may fail. This may lead to disappointment and they may stop making further attempts. But, if you learn the steps that are to be taken for achieving your goals, you will find things easy. Of course, you can not escape from taking the appropriate action but things may not be very difficult.

The first and foremost thing to succeed in achieving your objectives is that you should take complete responsibility of all your actions and the consequences there of. You must not blame others for your lapses nor should you be afraid to face the problems caused by your lapses. Before making any decision, you must weigh all the pros and cons, but, you should not unduly delay making your decision. Waiting for a perfect situation for commencing anything is a foolish attitude. Things can never be perfect. You should commence your action and can make the necessary corrections as you move along. Further, owning your mistakes and taking responsibility for your actions will improve your esteem in the eyes of others, hence, they themselves may come forward to help you to tide over the problems.

The most important weapon for success is to focus on your goal continuously and consistently. It is true that you may face road-blocks. However, these hurdles should not deter you from continuing to focus on your goals. Until your dreams are fulfilled, you should not lose sight of them. If an attempt fails, it maybe due to a mistake you commit in executing your plan or there may be something wrong with the plan itself. You should do an honest analysis. Find out the reason for the failure. Once you know the cause of the failure, you should take corrective action so that you are again on the right track for succeeding in your endeavors.

You should also find out your strengths and weaknesses. If you do an honest assessment, you will find that you will be focusing more on activities in which you are strong. You will have a tendency to postpone activities in which you are not very much comfortable. This attitude must be avoided. While you take steps to reinforce your strengths, you must take action to become strong in those areas in which you are weak. This will accelerate your success.

These are only a few steps. There are many other steps that should be taken for succeeding in life. You should first make a beginning for which you must make up your mind. "Dare to dream" is the advice of success gurus. Even for dreaming about success, you should have courage. Hence, you have to muster up enough courage to dream about success and work towards it.

CHAPTER 15

THE POWER OF PRAYER

When people need a breakthrough, they have no trouble asking God for help. Believers are taught to "make our requests known" through prayer. We understand that there is power in prayer and when you have an urgent need, you don't have time to wait. You need all the power that you can get.You need it fast! Right?

Unfortunately, too often, we fail to see that power work in a timely manner- if at all. How can that be? We are assured that God hears our prayers and is faithful to answer, right? So, what's the problem? Why don't get what we're asking God for when we need it?

To achieve your breakthrough, you must effectively use the power of prayer! You see, the power of prayer is not found solely spending time on your knees. Prayer can be done in the bed, in a closet, on the toilet. Whichever way you pray, it is just the beginning. It's like flipping the switch that sets a series of events in motion. It's the completion of those events that produces the results you desire. So here are four series of events that ignite the power of prayer and tap into your breakthrough.

1. Use the Word of God as the foundation

For your prayers to lead to the results, you have to know what to pray. God doesn't honor just any old request. This means you have to find the word on your particular situation. So, the first thing to do is answer the question, "God, what does your Word say about how is my situation is supposed to be?

    a.   How do I use this to help me get what I need?

2. A strong belief that God will provide

Most of the time we believe the Word is true for someone else but not for ourselves. You must convince ourself that His word is true not just for your family member, friend or neighbor but it's also true for you! There are two things to do to convince your brain that the Word works!

    a. Number one, you must constantly confess your belief in His Word. Speak the Word over and over and over and over. Everytime you have a thought contrary to His Word, counter that thought by speaking the Word out loud. Don't be afraid if others hear you.

    b. Number two, visualize the Word being true and manifesting. You have to see the breakthrough happening in your life. As you confess the it, picture

> it coming true. Engross yourself in that image as if you're already there. Feel every emotion that you'll experience when your break through arrives. Celebrate Mentally! Go ahead and start planning the party!

Okay, I got it. I am convinced that it is going to happen for me-not just someone else but me! Now what?

3. Actions that back up the belief for your breakthrough

The biggest mistake that limits the power of prayer and delays your breakthrough is lack of proper action after the prayer. We know that without faith it is impossible to please God. And, we know that faith is believing that He Can Do! What we forget or tend to discount is that there is work involved in having faith, for without works faith is dead. Now it's time to act like you know. How do you do that? If God says that He has provided for your needs then get busy finding out where he's keeping that provision.

But you say, what about waiting on God? What about it? When your house is on fire, do you sit in the living room waiting for God to put the fire out? Of course not! Then why sit around waiting on a miracle when your lights are about to get cut off or you're about to lose your home? Just because I'm busy doing what I can do within my power doesn't mean that .I'm not waiting on God. I'll be right where I'm supposed to be when He needs to get my miracle to me. In the meantime, I'm going to :

Ask

If you need money for basic needs or to keep from losing your car or house ask yourself, "What programs, services, etc. are available to people in this situation?" If you need a job ask, to see the hiring manager or find out where and how you can apply.

Seek

Seek out those who can lead you to or provide you with information that is valuable for what you need or where you desire to be. Surrounding yourself with people who have nothing in common with you hinders your progress.

Knock

Knock on the doors of those that can possibly help you and ask for what you are looking for. Find out, "Can you help me?" "Do I qualify?" If not, "Do you know someone who can?" Don't wait for God to magically drop the answer to your prayer in your lap. Get out of the house and find out where He's keeping your breakthrough!

By the time you get to this place. Your mindset should shift to know that you know. You know, without a shadow of a doubt, that you are on the right track. You are close to walking into your breakthrough.

And lastly,

4. Persistence In Faith For Your Breakthrough

Now of course there are times when you've done everything you know to do and still don't see your breakthrough. What do you do?

Be persistent in faith -that is, believing, and doing. No matter what it looks like, keep believing. Use the power of prayer and what you know about our loving God to combat very thought, emotion or feeling that tries to convince you when your breakthrough is not coming. Keep asking, "What else can be done? Keep seeking, "Who else can help?" Furthermore, keep knocking, "Where else can I go?" Before you know it, you will have your breakthrough and a whole lot more.

CONCLUSION

COMMITMENT

Commitment means being bound by a course of action to bring about the desired results. It is one of the most powerful personal traits that we can aim to achieve.

Our greatest leaders and the most successful business people all share common belief systems - determination, strength of purpose, and commitment.

Being committed to yourself, your goals, your business and your relationships is what raises you above the mediocre, because people who honor their commitments stand out in the crowd.

By honoring your commitments, you keep your promises and stay true to your word. Honoring your commitments also means that you promise to see them through to the very end, come what may. Not honoring your commitment destroys your credibility, dependability, and trust worthiness.

1. Commitment to Life

People who commit to living a successful, fulfilled life become the most successful, and fulfilled people.

Commitment is not simply about making a half-hearted promise to yourself that you may keep when "all the stars are aligned satisfactorily." Commitment involves making a promise to yourself that you will see through to the very end.

However, commitment doesn't mean following through on a goal for whatever reason becomes misaligned or doesn't prove to be the goal you originally wanted to achieve.

Making a promise that changes direction is entirely separate from breaking a promise.

To lead a fulfilled and happy life that raises you above the mediocre and clearly sets you on a path to achieve your life goals is what commitment is all about.

2. Commitment to Business

It would be impossible to imagine a business leader who doesn't value commitment as one of their greatest strengths.

Commitment requires courage, strength and perseverance. Personal traits find in any leadership manual.

Great business leaders not only practice commitment in their own lives, they encourage, promote and reward commitment in their employees.

Committed employees are competent and effective in the work place, as well as, being committed to the overall success and vision of the company.

Companies who engage in commitment in every facet of their organization raise themselves above the level of their competition by honoring their promises and fulfilling the needs of their customers.

3. Commitment to Success

Success doesn't just happen. Success occurs when determination, a desire to succeed, strength of purpose and a commitment to achieve your goals are present.

Successful people commit to achieving better than their best. For them, commitment becomes an instinctual habit they practice every day.

However, commitment is not merely about the intention or the strength of your promises, it is about taking action. Even the strongest commitment is just another broken promise unless a commitment to take action occurs.

Study the commonalities successful people possess. You will find at the heart of their success, a series of small and large goals that they work on with a determination to succeed and a commitment to go the distance.

4   Commitment to Relationships

You would swear from the number of books, seminars and workshops on the subject of "commitment phobia" that the phrase only belonged to the relationship game.

In fact, "commitment phobes" occur in all walks of life and are generally loathe to commit to anything.

Fulfilled and satisfying relationships form the backbone of our relationship with ourselves and the world around us.

Commitment to a relationship operates in the same way commitment to anything does.

Whether your relationship is personal, business, professional or sexual, committing to another individual is much the same as committing to an ideal or goal. You make a promise to that person and then you follow up with action.

Sounds simple, doesn't it? If so, then why do the statistics tell us that over 50% of marriages now end in divorce?

Human beings are amazingly complex creatures, so, the coming together of two complex creatures in an equally complex relationship can be fraught with mishaps, misunderstandings, doubt, deceit, despair...the list goes on.

In its most simplistic terms, committing to a relationship is no different from committing to a long term goal.   To stay committed, you need to keep your focus on the vision and understand that the path to attain that vision may meander, twist, turn, convolute and lead you down a number of dead ends. Nevertheless, stay committed.

About the Author

A native of Washington, D.C., **Andrée** overcame drug and alcohol abuse and temporary disability. While growing up, she witnessed domestic violence and used the arts to escape the trauma.

Andrée touches lives through books and films, some of which she uses to help people overcome complex challenges. As a transitional motivator, **Andrée** is continuously concerned with assisting people in mending from broken places and spearheading their lives upwards. **Andrée's** candid nature and transparency have been the window through which people can see that she genuinely cares. As a result of **Andrée's** desire to help others, she positively impacts as many people as possible within the U.S. and abroad.

In addition to hosting major events, 'Worthy Women of God and Keep it Real & Deal so Our Sisters Can Heal," **Andrée** began the 'Trust Your Transition' movement during Covid 19. This platform focuses on supporting the lives of individuals who are in transition. She has spoken at various venues and is the proud founder of Just 4 Us Foundation. **Andrée** supports non-profit organizations and assists in any philanthropic ventures that aim to help others. She has a passion for helping children with special needs or who are considered at-risk. She advocates for underprivileged children as she feels they are vital in making a difference in the world.

Andrée has nine children. Of the nine, she adopted seven (four are great-nieces and a nephew). Aside from her passion for children, her list of passionate special causes is foster care/adoption and domestic violence.

Andrée holds an Honorary Doctorate of Human Letters from Breakthrough Bible College. She is lovingly known to her peers as "The Evangelist of Lost Souls."

When Andrée is not filming, acting, writing, or speaking, she spends time with her children and grandchildren.

Her favorite motto is that "God can do anything but fail."

To find out more about **Andrée,** please visit her website at www.andreemharris.com.

To book **Andrée** for your event, contact info@andremharris.com

Social Media Platforms:

IG/Twitter/Snapchat/TikTok: iamandreeharris

Twitter: iamandreeharris

FB: **Andree M.** Harris

SnapChat/Tik Tok: iamandreeharris

andree@iamandreeharris.com

Made in the USA
Middletown, DE
16 July 2021